PASSENGER ON THE WINDRUSH

a play in two acts

by Dwight Marshalleck

As a boy, I watch the strong men and women
leave our village for England. They never
returned. Fifty years later, I tracked them
down in England. This is their tale of broken
promises, unrealized dreams, and love and loss
on London's streets.

-D.M.

Dedication

This Musical is dedicated to the folks who left the Caribbean to rebuild England, and even those who came aboard the "ship" in their "mammas' bellies". To the folks who told me their tales when I visited England, some of whom have passed on, I kept my promise. I kept my word.

Let no one deceive you with empty words,
because of these things the wrath of God comes
upon the sons of disobedience.
Ephesians 5:6

Acknowledgement

I could not have written this musical without the help of several of my friends. Thank you to my English family who welcomed me when I traveled to the UK to research this work. I am grateful to Naomi Sharland, who hosted me and introduced Junie James, the curator of the Windrush collection at Oxford University. Lorna and Merrick in Wolverhampton, you inspired my writing. My deepest gratitude to my niece Janice Marshalleck for directing me around England.

Rasta man Pablov Black, the great Studio One musician, thank you for believing my vision and my songs. I am indebted to my writing group; especially Sue, Pat, and Joe, for being patient, and encouraging me to sing pieces of this work. God is good to me for sending Eugene Grey to turn my songs into sheet music and soundtracks. Eugene without you, my story would be words on paper.

I am thankful to my editor, and friend, Philip Cross, who pushed me to "write like it's your last word." Philip, you know England well since you lived there during the Windrush years. If I did not mention any contributor by name, accept my sincere gratitude. I did not walk alone, but with your goodwill.

Redemption is never where you expect to find
it.
Sherrilyn Kenyon

<u>Cast of Characters</u>

<u>Papa Gilly</u>:	Reggae band leader
<u>Elaine Brown</u>:	Londoner from Caribbean parents
<u>Windham and Teddies</u>:	London gangsters
<u>Zekel</u>:	Caribbean expatriate
<u>Andrea</u>:	Singer and dance
<u>Reverend Deane</u>:	Anglican Minister
<u>Hark-Angel</u>:	Jamaican detective.
<u>Rudies</u>:	Dancers and singers
<u>Elder Matthews</u>:	Spiritual healer
<u>Becca</u>:	Windham's girl
<u>Calypsonian</u>:	
<u>Mento players</u>:	
<u>Latin singers</u>:	
<u>Edith-Louise</u>:	Woman on the ship
<u>Assistant detectives</u>:	
<u>Windrush Ship Captain</u>:	
<u>Windrush Crew</u>:	

<u>Scene</u>
Jamaica and London Streets

<u>Time</u>
1968 to 1973

ACT I

SCENE 1

SETTING: During the 20th anniversary of the Windrush, two sound systems clash at a local square. Reveling at a *send-off* party, a crowd celebrates "a chance of a lifetime" for folks leaving for London.

RISE: In center stage, girls in mini-skirts, men in gun-mouth pants are primed to dance the Ska. A single microphone perches in front. Oversized speakers stand beside a mural depicting men and women dressed, and ready to board the Windrush. All is set against an azure, cloud-capped Jamaican mountain.

PAPA GILLY

(raps from the echo chamber)

Now hear ye, this is a sound klash,
Dance like you po-cket full-a cash.
Two sound system unda heavy rhythm,
The best man win. Yeah, yeah yaay.

ANDREA AND THE RUDIES

(sing and dance)

Dis music is here to 1-a-st for-ever.
Rude bwoy gr-o-o-ve an' don't be cle-ver.
Rudies-show dem how to move their waist,
Swing your hips baby—jump out of your seat.

(After 30 seconds interrupts on the eco-
chamber)

PAPA GILLY
Hark it from the top to the very last drop.

ANDREA AND THE RUDIES (sing and dance)
Sound bwoy just ca'an handle the pace.
Every day dem cry an' drop out the race.
Tek this music to Buc-king-ham Pa-lac,
Swing your hips baby—we keep no malice.

Dis music is here to last for-ever.
Rude bwoys' groove don't be clev-er.
Girls show them how to move their feet,
Swing your hips baby—get out your seat.

PAPA GILLY

(toasts from the mike)

After a while,
Ska fell out of style.
You got to get ready,
This is Rock Steady.
Do it baby, do it.

ANDREA AND THE RUDIES
(sing and dance)

Smiles from loving eyes always get me dear.
That familiar feeling and I know you are here.
Your loving embrace, I will never, ever leave.
I give you my heart baby, do as you please.

Ships come to take me over the ocean, I fear.
I awake in your arms, and you dry every tear,
With your love, baby I will never, never leave.
I give you my heart baby, do as you please.

PAPA GILLY
(rap at the mike)

Here comes the tears of a broken heart.
Rock with me baby and we will never part.
Your lovin' embrace I will never, never leave.
I Give you my love, baby, do as you please.
Do it baby, do it.

(Hark Angel crashes the Party and accosts Papa Gilly.)

HARK ANGEL

Mash up this dance. It is I, Hark Angel-Messenger of Death from the Jamaica Constabulary Force. Shut down this sound-clash. Papa Gilly, I come for you ol' bwoy. You wanted for murder and manslaughter. When I appear, it is a bad day for the bad man. I am the Number one Bad-Man Police.
Papa Gilly, by the power invested in me by the New Prime Minister, the Governor General, and her Majesty, the Queen, I arrest you for murder.

PAPA GILLY

Who me? I killed no one. Hark Angel, you are
out to get me because your high school love is
now my woman. Why you want to mash up this
party? We are keeping a send-off party for our
people leaving for England. We are honoring
those who, over the years, left on the great
ship the Windrush.

HARK ANGEL

Hush. You are a singer in a band? Right? Where
is your big hit? You are just a DJ pretending
to be a singer. I will make sure you are tried
in the courthouse and hung by the neck on the
big cotton tree down by Ferry police station-
till you are dead. Papa Gilly, you will never
live to see your first-born child. Run away with
all these people going to England. Or make a
deal with me?

(sings)
I see your feet a-swinging.
From the big, big cotton tree.
Above the fields, green with sugar cane.

Papa Gilly, you Papa no-more.
Gi-lly you are Pa-pa no more.
You will never live to see your son.
I might shoot you now and put you out your
misery.
(draws gun and fires in the air)

ELDER MATTHEWS
Cease and desist all ye agents of Babylon. It
is I, Elder Matthews-spiritual reader, and
bush doctor in Jamaica. Leave Papa Gilly
alone. I draw a red line on this floor with
the blood of this African Sen-se Fowl. Hark
Angel, if you harm a strand of hair on Papa
Gilly's head, I will bring death and
destruction on your family for seven times
seven generations.

ELDER MATTHEWS
(chants to poco drums)
My herbs cure belly-ache an' fever.
I am better than a medical doctor.
Life's too hard, you ting don't work?
Come get you healing in my balm yard.

My herbs cure belly-ache an' fever.
I am better than a medical doc-tor.
Life's too hard, you ting don't work?
Come get you healing in my balm yard.

HARK ANGEL
(straddles the red line of blood)
Elder Matthews, your tom foolery don't
frighten me. I fear no man, magic or his
necromancy. Move out of my way or I will put
you out of business, Elder Matthews. I know
how your work. Trickery and scamming people
that you are a mind reader? I will expose you.

ELDER MATTHEWS
(Aside)
Brother Hark? Man, listen up. Tek it easy. I
don't want everybody to find out that I am not
really, really a mind-reader. Let us make
peace here. And when you leave, I have a big
ram-goat tie up by the side of my house. That
is your goat. Take the billy-goat and make a
big curry-goat feast for your friends. But let
Papa Gilly go. Do, my police brethren. [Aside]
You know police love freeness.

HARK ANGEL
(faces Elder Matthews)
What? Disrespecting a law officer? We bruck-up
bones and leave heads bloody.

ELDER MATTHEWS
I mean police love freedom of movement. People
are free go where they want without being
stopped by the police.

HARK ANGEL
Right. You better know your place Elder.
(addresses Papa Gilly:snare drums)

Run-way bwoy, don't ever look back.
I am never far, always on the clock.
Got you in my mighty paw,
The long arm of the law.

You might go underground.
Or run away to London town.
You cannot escape my claw,
The long arm of the l-a-w.

ANDREA
(split scene)
Papa Gilly, you must run away to England. My
father sent Hark Angel to kill you. People do
what Father commands. Gilly, I have been hiding
something from you. Gilly, I only turn sixteen
next week, you know. I love you.
PAPA GILLY
Sixteen Andrea? Like sweet sixteen?

ANDREA
I wanted to sing with you. In your band. But I
could not tell you I am under-age. I can't have
you; the father of my unborn baby get murdered
by Hark Angel.

PAPA GILLY
Unborn child? You pregnant Andrea? You said
you were nineteen? How come you never tell me?
How come Hark Angel know you are pregnant, and
I don't? He said I will never see my
firstborn.

ANDREA
You don't worry 'bout that. Everyone is leaving
for England. To get a better life. West Indians
have been going to England for decades and they
become rich up there. They send home barrels of
clothes and strong, strong English pounds to
their families in the islands. Go away to
England and send for me and our child to come
live with you.

PAPA GILLY
I am going nowhere. This is my born land.

ANDREA

For a better life Gilly. Go see the Englishman
Reverend Deane at my church. He will help you.
Kiss me before you go Gilly. I know you are
always travelling with your band. Will you be
true to me?

PAPA GILLY

True to you? I love you Andrea- Love of my life.
Even if I leave, I will return next month when
I get Hark Angel off my back. Wicked policeman.
Hmm. But I was dreaming about the big times.
Leave this little island and take my band on a
tour to London.

ANDREA

You do not know Hark Angel like I do. He is not
a forgiving man. Go to England and send for me.
Me and the Rudies will do a song for you. Carry
my music with you Gilly, in your heart. Never
forget me. The Rudies style will go with you
across the seas. Never forget.

(sings)
LOVE OF A LIFETIME

How can I, give up on love?
My-a-h love of a lifetime.
And I-ah feel you in my arms.
My l-o-ve of a life-time.

Ti-m-e stops- in your arms.
Nothin' but my beating heart.
Will you ever return-
Nothin' but my beating heart.

My love of a life-time
My love of a life-time
My love of a life-time

(Papa Gilly waits until night fall and races
to knock on Reverend Deane's door.)

                    PAPA GILLY
Reverend. I am in trouble. Big, big trouble. I
must escape. They are going to kill me. Hark
Angel…
          REVEREND DEANE (raises his hand)
Let's keep matters in perspective. Gilford is
your name, correct? I already know all that,
man. There are secrets of this island that
cannot elude a man of my intellect. Human
nature may be beyond your comprehension,
Gilford. I will tell you an extraordinary
secret, but you simply must never ever reveal
it. Hark Angel was trained in Scotland yard,
and he is secretly gay. He's got a thing for
you, man. After all you are indeed a fine-
looking chap.

                    PAPA GILLY
What you mean, gay? Really? He hates me and
threatens to hang me, but still, he has a
thing for me?

                  REVEREND DEANE
Son, this is Jamaica. Nobody, not even a high-
level policeman could possibly let it be known
he is a homosexual. That simply would be a
dreadful admission. Good God man, people would
stone him in the middle of the street.

                    PAPA GILLY
He is always persecuting me. Now he threatens
to kill me.

                  REVEREND DEANE

Those who persecute most fervently have an enormous guilt to conceal. Well then, a classmate of mine from Oxford might find the time to get you safely to England. Though the Windrush ship no longer sails to London, Great Britain still welcomes strong, healthy men like you to her friendly shores. The problem is though, I do not have the funds to assist you. Could you possibly find the wherewithal to purchase your airplane passage to England?

PAPA GILLY

Reverend Deane, I do not have a couple hundred English pounds for my airplane ticket. I must ask my uncle in the hills if he can sell one or two of his cows and raise the money for my ticket. I will pay him back later.

REVEREND DEANE

This is an enormous opportunity, a promise of a better life. Goodness Gracious me, go to England and see. Once you are there, pay me a visit when I return to London in the summer.

PAPA GILLY
(sings)
ON THE BRIDGE

*I am caught, oh on the bridge—feel—the
pressure on me.
Wrongfully accused, of a killing—feel the
pressure on me.
My life in the balance—yeah, my life in my
hands, oh Lord.
Leaving my unborn child—oh Lord, one foot in
the grave.*

I am caught on the bridge——in London Town.

Lawd I'd give my life for love—my Andrea.
I got to run—my pressure won't come down.
Hark angel, dark Angel, you will burn in fire.

I hide in the mist and the cold—London Town.

SCENE TWO

(London railroad yard laying down the tracks.)

PAPA GILLY

(monologue)

WHERE IS MY SUN?

Am I safe from the paw of the law?
Where is my sun, my orb of gold?
Big Ben chimes at the noon of day,
Still, she hides for time untold.
It's a fog over Westminster way.
Damp and chilling, dark and brooding.

Is this summer, or the horrid winter of my
discontent, possibly?
My bed and pillow set low on the floor of the
Seaman's Infirmary.
Yes, I board at the Seaman's syphilis hospital
in Clapham.
They house me like a leftover from the war—a
madman.
Andrea, my love back o'er the Caribbean Sea—
out of sight.
My plight employed to rebuild Britain's great,
great might.

And I like Faust hath sold my soul for a great
cost.
Andrea and my unborn child, all is gone, all
is lost.
Huge chimneys on houses belching smoke like
factories.
To be with my Andrea, I would trade the
queen's riches.
Where is my sun? No sun, no golden sun.
A fog-damp and chilling, dark and brooding.

TEDDIES

Shad up Golliwag. Rubbish. Rubbish. Nig-nog.
Mind your mouth scum before I bash your head,
bam.
Hustle up then. Return to the dead-yard in
Clapham.
I'll have the Home Office here to drag you out
by the ear.
Bloody well run you off to your coconut isle
way out there.
For now, bend your backs to get the railroad
up and running.
Trains will dart through with the
stationmaster announcing:
This is the Piccadilly Line, the Blue Line to
Cockfosters.
Next stop Piccadilly Circus. Revel in
England's treasures.
Mind the gap. Yah here ah.

PAPA GILLY

Teddies in their Doc Marten boots, swinging
their chairs, and threatening. Is this why I
came to this country?

WIDNHAM AND THE TEDDIES
(sings)

Nig-Nog look.
You're not light like Portland cement,
Not even a legal resident.
You rebuild for the next Jubilee.
London is big, a city for the celebrity.
Rebuilding like the Phoenix after the War.
By my knuckle-duster, Sambo, I am a star.

Rebuilding done, go back to your fun.
Oh, island in the sun, your golden sun.
No sun can burn through our London fog.
Someone go on fetch me a proper cup.

Hot tea never lasts past the first sup.
Britain lasts a thousand years and up.

BECCA
Windham, you are not a politician.
But goodness me, you do sound like the famous
one.

TEDDIES
Britain reigns a thousand years by any shot.
Much longer than the fate of this cursed lot.

(sing)
You are not light as Portland cement.
We can't make you a legal resident.
Rebuilding for the great, great Jubilee
London is a big city for the ce-leb-rity.
A Phoenix rising from the great, great War.
Sambo, I am big star, Sambo, I am big star.

RUDIES
Kool it, Mate. You are good at war, conquest,
and stuff like that. But human spirit rebuilds
after you blokes "mash up" things and get
depressed. Let's get this place lit.
(sings)
ISLAND MOVES
London mash up after your big bad war.
England cry out come from near and far.
Goodness Gracious, offer of a lifetime.
Leave the colonies, chance of lifetime.
You need our spirit to get this place lit.
Island move, body groove, get this place lit.

Move over and let us turn London to bright.
Even if you are cement white, get right.
London mash up after your big bad war.
England cry out come from near and far.

You need our spirit to get this place lit.
Island moves, body grooves, get this place
lit.

SCENE THREE

(After work above ground. Teddies loafing at
the Pub.)

TEDDIES

You wanna fight Mate? Yes? Grovel if you must
but make no fuss. We bash darkies like you. Ya
hear ah?

RUDIES
(sing and dance)

You need our spirit to get this place lit.
Island moves, body grooves, get this place
lit.

You need our spirit to get this place lit.
Island moves, body grooves, get this place
lit.

PAPA GILLY
(sings)
BORN WITH A TAN

Mamma gave me this tan.
Draped in melanin like a sapphire night
without a moon.
It don't mean, I got no feelin', deep in my
soul.
Oh, I can work all night and day without
breaking.
I got this feeling for my wo-man left weeping.
On a sapphire night, without a moon.
Ooh my love, w-a-i-t I'll come soon.

Night and day, I am grieving, in her arms I'd
be rejoicing.
This labor would be light as the island breeze
a-blowing.
And wouldn't I toil as hard as they please? As
hard...

I see my child in my woman's arms.
She is standing where I left her.
On a sapphire night, without a moon.
Ooh my love, w-a-i-t, I'll come soon.

TEDDY BOY'S RESPONSE
(sings)
PORTLAND CEMENT
You are not light as Portland cement.
You are only a bloody illegal resident.
Rebuilding for the great, great Jubilee
London is a big city for the ce-lebr-ity.

You can't drink with us. No. Not even a bloody
pint
Nig-Nog. Go home unless you want a dreadful
fight.
Unless you want a dreadful fight, a dreadful
fi-g-ht.

RUDIES
(confront and sing)
Move over and let us turn London bright.
Even if you are cement white, get right.
London mash up after your big bad war.
England cry out come from near and far.
You need our spirit to get this place lit.
Island move, body grove, get this place lit.
Ah suh wi dweet.

WORKER ZEKEL
(Approaches Papa Gilly)
Teddy Boys, we soon fix your business. You
just come to London, bloke? You look
frightened. Hear this. Teddies are the biggest
terrorists of black people in England. We Rude
Bwoys have been tussling with Teddies for
twenty years. Now is the time to wipe them
out.

(Raps to drumbeat)
*Every day we walk in packs to catch the
homebound trains.
Them Teddy Boy gangs will beat you with their
wire chains.
Take this long screwdriver and never
surrender.
I always carry one in my pocket just remember.
Rude bwoys fight for justice and never
surrender.*

Make sure you are never alone. Link up with us
Rudies. Do not walk alone. Ever. Mi name
Zekel. Yes. I came on the first Windrush in
1948. I will help you to wipe out them
Teddies.

PAPA GILLY
(coughing)

A big, long, sharp screwdriver? Thanks man. I
am Papa Gilly. It is supposed to be spring, and
it is cold as rass. Filthy snow banked up on
the side of the road. Will it snow again
tonight? I came here for a better life, but I
am developing asthma. You hear my chest
wheezing in that dirty factory air. I don't know
how long I can take this hostile environment.

ZEKEL

Are you unwell? London can have four seasons in
one day. You don't got a jacket. You got nothing
bloke? I was watching you today. You can't
really manage this job of putting down the
tracks. Here is an extra sweater. Bundle up man.

PAPA GILLY
Zekel, Thanks brother. I was a music teacher
back in Jamaica. Never pick up a sledgehammer
in my life. You know I went to the schoolhouse
here to apply for a job. They told me, "No way
you can be a teacher. Blacks can't be
teachers."

ZEKEL
Bullies pick on loners, Papa Gilly. Caribbean
people are teaming up and pooling their money.
We call it "throwing partner". Every week I
contribute money with a pool of friends. Once
a month one member gets the draw and use the
money to buy a house. My turn to get the draw
soon come. I am buying my own home soon.

PAPA GILLY
You doing good, man. When will I ever buy my
own house in London?

ZEKEL
Anyway we done work for the day. Let's get out
this dungeon.

PAPA GILLY
Every morning, as I leave the place where I
lodge, the bloke from the night shift walks in.
That bloke gets in the same iron bed I just got
out of. Did I keep the mattrass warm for him?
You know that old nursery rhyme?
Room for rent apply within
When I run out you run in.
                    (They laugh)
The bloke's name is Mr. Box.

ZEKEL

We should call you Mr. Cox like in the tale of
the English landlady who collects double rent.
The lady rents the same bed to Mr. Box during
the day and then the same bed to Mr. Cox at
night.
(They laugh)
Tales of the English. How did we get here? On
a promise of a better life? Right Mr. Cox?

TEDDY BOY

Bus is coming. Ya here ah. Go back to your
bunk bed in the infirmary down Clapham
Southside. Yah can't get any flats here. See
the signs:
Room for rent apply within.
No Dogs, No Irish, No Blacks.

SCENE 3

(flashback projection of the Windrush ship)
ZEKEL

Teddies still messing with us after all this
time in London. Papa Gilly let me tell you
about the trip on the original Windrush. The
fellows from the islands brought their musical
instruments and the English captain let us
play in the evenings. We partied all night
when we could. Day and night, we dreamed of
making England our new home.

CALYPSONIAN

(sing)

COME TO LONDON AND SEE

England welcomes you to her friendly shore.
See a smiling face as you go door to door.
Goodness Gracious, come to London and see
Chance of a lifetime, Goodness Gracious me.
Great Britain is a place I'm longing to see.

I going to Cambridge to be an engineer.
Have no fear, you are welcome over here.
Goin' to Queen's hospital, a nurse I'll be.
Goodness Gracious me, come to London and see.
Chance of a lifetime, Goodness Gracious me.

Have a sip of de Bajan rum,
Dance, but don't tumble down.
Have no fear, you are welcome over here.
Goodness Gracious me, come to London and see.
A chance of a lifetime, Goodness Gracious me.

ZEKEL

On the ship I took a fancy to Edith-Louise, a
young lady form Barbados. Her skin was like
the color of a valley just before dusk turns
the night pitch dark. She wanted to become a
nurse in England.

EDITH-LOUISE

Why don't you come dance with us behind these
speakers.

ZEKEL

Aren't you back there wukking it up with your
man?

EDITH-LOUISE

No man, just my cousins? I am Edith-Louise.

ZEKEL

Edith-Louise I wanted to beg you for a dance
all night.

EDITH-LOUISE

I know that. I saw you staring at me. You
almost tripped on your two big feet every time
you pass. You have two left feet? (chuckles)

ZEKEL AS MENTO SINGER
(sings)
THE VALLEY AT DUSK

You dance like waves rolling to the shore.
I swing with your moves and beg for more.
Light touches your skin, soft as a valley at
dusk
I reach out and touch, soft as a valley at
dusk.

We dance like waves rolling to the shore.
We swing and dance and search for more.

Light touches your skin, soft as a valley at
dusk.
I hold you, soft as the grass in the valley at
dusk.

You dance like waves rolling to the shore.
I swing with your moves and beg for more.
Light touches your skin, soft as a valley at
dusk.
I reach out and touch, soft as a valley at
dusk.

ZEKEL

One month on a ship, you know Papa Gilly is a
long time. I could not stand to be apart from
her. I sneaked into her cabin every night and
left before daylight. On a gray afternoon we
spotted London on the horizon. We ran to the
deck to catch a glimpse of the city. The ship
sailed up the Thames to dock at Tilden Yard

LATIN SONG
(sings to Pachucco Boogie)

How can I, give up on love?
My-a-h love of a lifetime.
And I-ah feel you in my arms.
My l-o-ve of a life-time.
Ti-m-e stops- in your arms.
Nothin' but my beating heart.

Will you ever return-
Nothin but my beating heart.
My love of a life-time
My love of a life-time
My love of a life-time.
Nothin but my beating heart.

SHIP CAPTAIN
(interrupts with Klaxon horn)

Ar-Ar. Attention. Silence on the aft. Quiet on deck. Get ready for docking at Tilden Yard. Shut down that irreverent music. Put away those boisterous instruments and hold steady for docking. You heah? Ah!

ACT II
SCENE 1

(London Street scene. Walking home after
work.)

PAPA GILLY

Zekel, for five years I have been working with
the blokes in the railyard. I am moving out of
the old syphilis hospital where they lodge us
in Clapham Southside. Twenty of us to a room
sleeping in bunk beds.

ZEKEL

I was supposed to go to college and study to
study be an engineer. Look at me now. Twenty
years ago, when I began working underground, I
could pick up this railroad tie by myself. Now
after working all day, I can barely pick up my
supper at night.
(They chuckle)

PAPA GILLY

You know, I had my own house in Jamaica. Now I
lay at night thinking of my woman and my baby
back in Jamaica.

ZEKEL

A woman, good or bad is hard to find here. I
had a white woman once. Her brother grabbed
her and beat her bloody for going with me.
Tortured her. I miss my black woman whom I met
on the Windrush. She was beautiful and brown
as the hills at twilight. Edith-Louise is her
name. I wonder where she is. Never saw her
after we left the ship—love her to bits.
(Sings)
WORTH IT
If I ever—hold you again—fill my heart with
your love.

The thunder of hammers and the smell of
burning oil
Would cease, and my heart aches no more for
your love.
Brown cocoa skin—twilight on my lonely, lonely
hills.
And this toil in the dungeon of my soul would
be worth it.
Some d-a-y I will see you again and life would
be worth it.

(Tosses his hat and sits on the railroad tie.)
For years, I searched all of England for the
love of my life. As soon as I save up enough
pounds, I will trot off to find my her again,
after all this time. My Edith-Louise…
                    (sings)
Brown cocoa skin—twilight on my lonely, lonely
hills.
And this toil in the dungeon of my soul would
be worth it.
Some-day I'll see you again and my life would
be worth it.
If I ever—hold you again—I'll fill my heart
with your love
My thunder ceases, and my heart aches no more
for your love.
And my life would be worth it, and life would
be worth it.

(Zekel: tosses his jacket aside and plops
                    down)
I wanted to fight for my rights like a Rude
bwoy. But now I have lost out on love and
life, and I am too old to be a Rude bwoy or a
fighter. Pappa Gilly, I have a secret. I am
not really from Jamaica. I is from Trinidad.
Yes, I am Trini.

PAPA GILLY
(puts his arm around Zekel)
I have always known that Zekel. I understand
old chap. But once a Rude bwoy, always a Rudey.
Yesterday I got a telegram from my own woman
back in Jamaica. Says, "Urgent, your daughter
is sick. Send money." I would prefer to leave,
but now I must work harder and send money home.
But the little pay I get is pocket money. Come
now Zekel. You a good fellow. Put your hat on
before you catch pneumonia. Let us walk to see
Reverend Deane. I know him from Jamaica. He has
a church nearby, and there is a pretty girl
rehearsing for their spring variety concert. I
want to meet her.

(Zekel picks up the railroad tie and they walk
towards the back, where Zekel tosses the
railroad tie to rumbling echo.)

ZEKEL
Last time I went to church in London the
minister said, "My gratitude to you for
coming, but do not return. You hear fellow.
Your kind of people are not welcome here."
What that tells you? We must form our own
house of worship to combat all this racial
prejudice. Hear that voice inside the church?

FEMALE SINGER (ELAINE)
(sings)
JERICHO ROAD
Sometimes you take the train down Jericho
Road.
Rebuilding the Great Empire is such a heavy
load.
The lodging they offer is the Seaman's
infirmary.

There is no room in the inn, no room in the
city.
Let not your heart be troubled on this dark
day.
God knows your name and will make a way.

Make your way through the dark and gloom.
My God is bringing light into this very room.
A Phoenix rising, through the fog London—town
Rising through the fire and ash of London
town.

Rebuilding the Great Empire is a heavy load.
There is no room in the inn, no rest in the
city.
Can't lay my head in the sick man's infirmary.
Oh-oh oooh the train down to Jericho Road.

Let not your heart be troubled on this dark
day.
My God knows your name and will make a way.
There is a Phoenix rising up from the ashes.
Up from the dust into the new London Town.

SCENE TWO

(meets girl (Elaine) singing at the rehearsal)
PAPA GILLY
Reverend Deane, who is that young lady with
the angelic voice. Her eyes are big and
beautiful. She looks like a star.

REVEREND DEANE
That is Elaine Brown. She is a nurse with the
National Health Service. Our church is
rehearsing for an Easter Revival, and we
invited her to sing. She has her own gospel
band.

PAPA GILLY
Can I meet her? I been having dreams about
her.

REVEREND DEANE
Good God Man, don't you have a woman left back
in Jamaica? Isn't this a bit of betrayal?

PAPA GILLY (dismisses the Reverend)
Betrayal Reverend? What about my promise of a
better life now turned into a sentence in the
tombs of the railroad?
Ah! Yes but... Can I sing with Elaine Brown and
her band? Just a little tune I am feeling.

(Sings)
LOVE SURPRISE
Aw, Aw love comes as a sur- pr-i-se
Aw, aw fell for those beautiful eyes.
Aw, aw never, never knew you would care.
Aw, aw, love flows here there and everywhere.

Aw, Aw love comes as a sur- pr-i-se
Aw, aw fell for that beautiful smile.
Aw, aw never, never you would care.
Aw, aw love flows here, there, and everywhere.

People dancing in the street.
Everybody rocking to the beat.
(rap)
You body, you body movable,
Shake it, make it rumble.
Unzip it, and mek it tumble.

ELAINE
You got style. I quite like that. You never
been in a band?

PAPA GILLY

It is a long story. I had my own band. That is why they call me Papa Gilly. Elaine, your singing reminds me of a certain Jamaican singer, Phyllis Dillon. She is my inspiration. How about we meet for a proper cup of tea after the show? I will tell you, my story.

ELAINE

Excellent. I only drink the finest tea. Can you possibly meet me at the tea shop close to Westminster Bridge? You know where that is, Jamaican Man?

PAPA GILLY

I know that place. [Aside] Zekel, can you take me to that fine Tea-shop?

ZEKEL

Upscale place. Barely know it myself. You can't wear that dirty work clothes down there. But come, we buy a shirt on the way, and jump on the Tube. We can get to the Bridge before she takes off her fancy makeup and drive in her limousine. She is too "high society" for you, but I know in "matters of the heart" folks lose their senses and get above their head.

SCENE THREE

(meets girl at tea shop near Westminster Bridge)

ZEKEL

I will take a few winks on this park bench. Call me if you need me. You have your long screwdriver? Teddies are still about looking for trouble.

TEDDY BOY'S RESPONSE
(sings)
PORTLAND CEMENT
You are not light as Portland cement.
We are only a bloody illegal resident.
Rebuilding for the great, great Jubilee
London is big, city for the celebrity.

RUDIES RESPONSE
(sings)
ISLAND GROOVES
You need our spirit to get this place lit.
Island moves, body groves, get this place lit.

Move over and let us turn London to bright.
Don't care you are cement white, get right.
London mash up after your big bad war.

ELAINE
(enters)
You know there is protest going about the
Windrush scandal. They are deporting people,
calling them illegal aliens. England has now
become a hostile environment for people who
helped rebuild her. You have your English
citizenship?

PAPA GILLY
No, I am a proud Islander. I care nothing for
an English citizenship. I came here on the
five-year plan to earn some money and return
home and finish building my house. What about
you?

ELAINE

My mother is from Barbados, and she met my
father on the Windrush. He came from Trinidad,
and he wanted to go to college and study to be
an engineer. One long month on a ship, you
know things happen. I came in my Mamma belly
on the original Windrush in 1948.

PAPA GILLY

Whaat? You were conceived on the Windrush?

ELAINE

They were supposed to get married, but the
Department for Work sent him all over the
country to work on railroads. They could not
find each other. She suffered alone. I was
born right here in London University Hospital.
Imagine that, my father a railroad man that I
never met, and now I am falling for you a
railroad man.

PAPA GILLY

Am I so bad? Working her majesty's railroad
track?

ZEKEL
(Aside)

Her mother a nurse? On the Windrush? From
Barbados? Could she be my daughter? Naah. Ask
her what was her mother's name? Silly boy.
Edith Louise? Edith-Louise. Brown cocoa skin?

ELAINE

Hmm. In time, Mamma married a bus driver.
Mamma is a nurse, as am I. Nurses built the
National Healthcare Service for England. We
are like the legendary nurse Mary Seacole. She
got no recognition for her long service to the
Empire as well. I am torn between my loyalty
to the Caribbean and England, the country of
my birth.

PAPA GILLY

Elaine, five years come and gone, and I feel
every penny I earn falls in a sink hole. Now
that we are done rebuilding everything, they
trot out this hostile environment. They say,
"We own these people, and by George, we shall
send them home when done with their labor."

ELAINE

We Barbadians did not have to leave home to
help rebuild Britain. Our economy is strong.
But nurses have a good life here in Britain,
though. I did not have to struggle like you
folks—putting six pence in the meter to get
hot water. Or paying to use the outdoor
latrine.

PAPA GILLY

Well, I had to run for my life from Jamaica,
but I was the leader of a reggae band.
Police...

ELAINE

What did you do? Women worries, right? You are
a handsome chap.

PAPA GILLY

Women worries, money worries, and problems. A murderous policeman set me up because of his love fantasies with me. Imagine that? I don't want to lose my Jamaican man card over a man. Who does he think I am?

ELAINE

Yes, we know. There is no love between men in Jamaica. That is if you want to keep your life. Only secret love among men.

PAPA GILLY

Elaine, how you know suh?

ELAINE

I know things. Female intuition. Gilly, I shan't call you Papa. I know that you have taken a fancy for me, Gilly. (Gets up and paces) You know, fallen for me, and I quite like that. Drink up. Hot tea never last in London. Just like moments of our lives.

PAPA GILLY
(walks towards her)

A moment is all it takes, and suddenly the London April showers cease. And we are in the summer of our love.

ZEKEL
(aside)

Hmmm. Hot tea? Moments? Nothing ever lasts. Nothing. Gilly, I think she is a better class than us railroad men. And she could be my daughter.

PAPA GILLY

Aw shadupp Zekel. Quiet. What do you know
about matters of the heart. You have given up
on love a long time ago. Let us have a proper
time.

ZEKEL

Ay bloke, 1 will take you to a Blues Dance in
Battersea. Yes Man. Show you how to have a
proper time in a basement party. You will be
wearing your finest jacket and tie. Hear
Lloydie Coxsone, King of dub rock at the
turntable. Teddies cannot make moves like
this-dancing to Desmond Dekker and the Aces.
You won't see a white man down there. However,
you will see white girls dancing with their
black men in a dark corner. If you can't stand
the stinking ganga smoke, don't go to a Blues
Dance.

PAPA GILLY

You know that I love my ska and Rock Steady
music. Can we bring Elaine? When can we go,
Zekel?

ZEKEL

We will go this Friday. You can have a proper
pint, or two. You better bring your own woman
because if you see a lady dancing alone, don't
plead with her to have a dance. Be polite. Her
man is watching you. If you touch his woman-
big fight will break out.

ELAINE

Gilly come over heah. You and I will do excellent things together. I am already a well-known singer in the church circles. I know my Island music-like Honey Boy, and John Holt. I want to break into the Lover's Rock market. The English version of what you Jamaican Rude Bwoys call Rock Steady. You know... singing tunes like the one you did at the church.
(they sing together)

Aw, aw Love comes as a surprise.
Aw, aw fell for those beautiful eyes.
Aw, aw Look into those beautiful eyes.
(they giggle and kiss)

PAPA GILLY

Reggae is hard to break into for women. If you are ready to break that mold, I will help you. You know I had my own band back in Jamaica.

(sings)
MAN'S MUSIC

Reggae's a man's music; Reggae's a man's music.
A woman's voice don't fit with this acoustic.
Can you leave church, sing with the Rude Bwoys?
Lost, grumpy men who never had nice, nice toys.
Can you wear a mini-skirt and swing your hips?
No church music from your sugar, sweet lips.

Reggae's a man's music; Reggae's a man's music.
You make people dance— your voice of magic.
Can you wear a mini-skirt and swing your hips?
No more church music from your sweet, sweet lips.

(rap)

Now I can stop my search.
I am taking you out of church.
Found a love that I can feel.
My life here just became real.

ELAINE
I got this. Listen this.
(sings)
WOMAN'S MUSIC
*Reggae's woman's music; Reggae's woman's
music.
A woman's voice flows with this kinda
acoustic.
I can sing better than your rude, Rude Bwoys.
Lost, grumpy men who never had nice, nice
toys.
I can wear a mini-skirt and swing my saucy
hips.
And sing reggae music from my sugar, sweet
lips.*

*Reggae's a woman's music; Reggae's woman's
music.
We make people dance—with our voices of
magic.
I can wear a mini-skirt and swing my saucy
hips?
Sing all kinds of music from my sugar-sweet
lips.
A woman's voice can play with any style
acoustic.
I can sing with better than your rude, Rude
Bwoys.*

(rap)
*Now I can stop my search.
We can stay in the church.
Found a love that I can feel.*

My life here just became real.

PAPA GILLY
Well, we danced all night, and I must go to
work in that dungeon.

ELAINE
Gilly, here is my scarf. It is a Burberry. The
finest in the world. Wear it, Lovie, and
think of me when you go underground. Kiss me
once more Gilly. Will you be my sweetheart?
You are not a runner, are you a Rude Bwoy?
(departs stage)

ZEKEL
Daylight soon come. We need to get back on
the tracks before the Teddies start looking
for us, Gilly. I did not even eat a biscuit
for breakfast. But I know you up all night
kissing. Maybe she is too good for you
Railroad Man. You not really a singer anyway.
Just a deejay.

SCENE THREE

(underground railroad track)
PAPA GILLY
To be with a woman like that? To have and to
hold my own? I have been in London five years
now, and usually I am really gutted when I
must go underground. Not today! Today it is
worth it Zekel.

ZEKEL
Nice scarf. You smell good too. The smell of
woman. Oh, how I miss my Edith- Louise, my
love.

TEDDIES
Mind yourself yah hear ah. What are you doing
with a Burberry scarf around your neck? Fetch
it to me so that I can wipe mi arse.

PAPA GILLY
You come over here and touch my scarf and I
run this long screwdriver through your belly.

TEDDY BOY'S RESPONSE
(sing)
You are only a bloody illegal resident.
Work, hustle, or home you'll be sent.
Rebuilding for the great, great Jubilee
London is big city for the celebrity.
    (Teddy Boy grabs the scarf and sniffs.)

TEDDIES
Smell like woman's bloomers, high-end perfume.
You have fancy woman Nig-Nog. I wouldn't wipe
my ass with this cloth. I will trample it in
the mud and then you can wear it.
(Tussle breaks out. Papa Gilly brandishes his
long screwdriver.)

PAPA GILLY

Yes, my woman gave this scarf to me. Blood and
fire now. We Rude Bwoys. We fight oppression.

TEDDY BOYS

Aah. Bloody Hell. You stab me in the arm.
Call the Bobbies to lock your arse up. The
Home office will get rid of you. Send you back
home to your coconut island.

(Police come and drag Papa Gilly to the
holding cell)

PAPA GILLY
(sings)
LONDON RAIN

Just when I found the looo-ve of my life,
Here comes the rain--London rain,
All over broken, broken heart.
I reach for you babe, and you flit away
Here comes the rain, London rain,
All over my broken, broken heart.

Shadows come like rain London rain,
All over my broken, broken heart.
It rains, like London rain.
Just when I found the love of my life,
Here come the rain, London rain,
London pain, all over by broken heart.

Here come the rain, London rain
London pain, all over by broken heart.

(Elaine come to bail him out. Spotlight on
Papa Gilly behind jail bars.)

ELAINE

Rude bwoy you get in trouble? Sorry it took me
a week, but they could not find me. I was in
the studio making a new record. Yes, a Rock
Steady tune. I am here to save my Rude Bwoy.
Look the sun is out.

PAPA GILLY

I used the week to write you a song, Elaine—
Babe.

(sings)
A GOLDEN SUN

*A golden sun
Yes, finally sun.
It is the light.
Your beautiful eyes*

*You light my way.
Am I here to stay?
More than today
Our golden sun*

*I close my eyes.
When I lost my way,
No light of day
But your beautiful smile.*

*Don't look away,
My brand-new day,
Love shows the way.
Am here to stay.*

ELAINE

I understand the plight of the man working on
the tracks. Teddies always terrorizing you.
My daddy worked as a bus driver and saved up
to purchase a car. He made the mistake of
telling his boss. Next thing you know, they
fired him. I understand why you Rude Bwoys
always fight for your rights. Gilly, dearest.
Just stop. Hear my new Lover's Rock song on
the radio?

(sings rocksteady song)
RUDE BWOY WALK

Babe-e-eh
I love your rude bwoy way of walking.
Babe-e-eh
And your Jamaican way of dancing.
But if you are going to be my lover yeah,
You must make me tingle all over babeh
Babe-e-eh
Just give me the finer things of life,
If you want me to be your wife?

Babe-e-eh
I can't be your secret lover,
Y-a-a-y
You can't keep me under cover.
Wo-wow- a-a-a-y
Rude Bwoy, walking.
Rude Bwoy talking.

Babe-e-eh
I am good under the cover.
Yeah
Can y-o-u be my lover?

Babe-e-eh
You must love my rude girl style
Babe-e-eh
You feel my passion all the while?

Yaaay
A girl has a right to claim her love.
Baby I am best anytime you need me.
My Rude Bwoy can you ever love me?

PAPA GILLY

Elaine you are a big hit now. A celebrity.
Lover's Rock gone clear. English bands
imitating our music. Stinger is copying our
style and his version of Lover's rock is
number one on the British charts. Rodigan is
playing your songs all over England.

ELAINE

I know. Another group "We B 50"is making a
cover album of Lover's rock and reggae. Now
the Home Office is coming to deport you. Just
as I found you, the love of my life.

(Home Immigration officers arrive to deport
Papa Gilly.)
TEDDIES

Immigration, Immigration—scatter, flatter,
Birds of a feather flock together,
Live together, then leave together.
To your "Oh, island in the sun."
Hostile environment, our government.
   (Crowd protests the deportation. Hark Angel
                arrives from Jamaica)

HARK ANGEL

I come to escort you home at the behest of Her
Majesty. The long arm of the law always gets
you.
You might to the devil sell your soul,
But today, for you the bells must toll.
 (Constabulary band performs to when we all get
                to heaven)

FOREIGN LAND

When you return from foreign land,
No one awaits to shake your hand.
Bring a suitcase full of money,
Do, don't mashup, the country.
Yes sah, the pound strong,
Stronger the weak Jamaican dollar.

Deportees get no seven-gun salute.
You mess with the queen, my youth.
Yes sah, the pound strong in the island.
Yes sah, the pound strong in this land.
Rude Bwoy, do, keep your record clean.
My youth don't mess with England Queen.

ELAINE

(Opens the jail door)
Come Rude Bwoy. I come to get you, Lovie.

(Signals STOP and the finale is a dance truce
between the Teddies and the Rudies)

TEDDIES

(sing)
DON'T BE PORTLAND CEMENT

You don't have to be light like Portland
cement.
Rude bwoy, you were al-ways a welcome
resident.
Rebuilding for the great, great Jubilee
London is a big city for the ce-leb-rity.
A Phoenix rising from the great, great War.
Windrush people you are stars, big, big stars.

I don't have to be light like Portland cement.
Rude girl, you were al-ways a welcome
resident.Rude Bwoys Rebuilding for the great
Jubilee,
London is a big, big city for the ce-leb-rity.

Windrush people we are stars, big, big stars.
Windrush people we are stars, big, big stars.

RUDIES

(Rudies sing and dance variation of Portland Cement)
London mash up after your big bad war.
England cry out come from near and far.
Goodness Gracious, offer of a lifetime.
Leave the colonies, chance of lifetime.

You need our spirit to get this place lit.
Island move, body groove, get this place lit.

Move over and let us turn London to bright.
Even if you are cement white, get right.
London mash up after your big bad war.
England cry out come from near and far.

You need our spirit to get this place lit.
*Island moves, body grooves, get this place
lit.*

(curtains close)

1. RUDIES GROOVE

ANDREA AND THE RUDIES
(sing and dance)
Dis music is here to l-a-st for-ever.
Rude bwoy gr-o-o-ve an' don't be cle-ver.
Rudies-show dem how to move their waist,
Swing your hips baby—jump out of your seat.

(After 30 seconds interrupts on the eco-chamber)

PAPA GILLY
Hark it from the top to the very last drop.

ANDREA AND THE RUDIES
(sing and dance)
Sound bwoy just ca'an handle the pace.
Every day dem cry an' drop out the race.
Tek this music to Buc-king-ham Pa-lac,
Swing your hips baby—we keep no malice.

Dis music is here to last for-ever.
Rude bwoys' groove don't be clev-er.
Girls show them how to move their feet,
Swing your hips baby—get out your seat.

2. LOVING EYES
ANDREA AND THE RUDIES
(sing and dance)

Smiles from loving eyes always get me dear.
That familiar feeling and I know you are here.
Your loving embrace, I will never, ever leave.
I give you my heart baby, do as you please.

Ships come to take me over the ocean, I fear.
I awake in your arms, and you dry every tear,
With your love, baby I will never, never leave.
I give you my heart baby, do as you please.

PAPA GILLY
(toasts at the mike)

Here comes the tears of a broken heart.
Rock with me baby and we will never part.
Your lovin' embrace I will never, never leave.
I Give you my love, baby, do as you please.
Do it baby, do it.

After a while.
Ska fell out of style.
You got to get ready,
This is Rock Steady.
Do it baby, do it.

3. POLICE JAM

(Hark Angel sings)

I see your feet a-swinging.
From the big, big cotton tree.
Above the fields, green with sugar cane.

Papa Gilly, you Papa no-more.
Gi-lly you are Pa-pa no more.
You will never live to see your son.

4. ELDER MATTHEWS' CHANT

My herbs cure belly-ache an' fever.
I am better than a medical doctor.
Life's too hard, you ting don't work?
Come get you healing in my balm yard.

My herbs cure belly-ache an' fever.
I am better than a medical doc-tor.
Life's too hard, you ting don't work?
Come get you healing in my balm yard.

5. MIGHTY PAW OF THE LAW
(Hawk Angel raps)

Run-way bwoy, don't ever look back.
I am never far, always on the clock.
Got you in my mighty paw,
The long arm of the law.

You might go underground.
Or run away to London town.
You cannot escape my claw,
The long arm of the l-a-w.

6. LOVE OF A LIFETIME
(Andrea and the Rudies)

How can I, give up on love?
My-a-h love of a lifetime.
And I-ah feel you in my arms.
My l-o-ve of a life-time.

Ti-m-e stops- in your arms.
Nothin' but my beating heart.
W-ill you ever re-turn-
Nothin' but my beating heart.

My love of a life-time,
My love of a life-time,
My love of a life-time.
Nothin' but my beating heart.

7. ON THE BRIDGE
Papa Gilly

I am caught, oh on the bridge—feel—the
pressure on me.
Wrongfully accused, of a killing—feel the
pressure on me.
My life in the balance—yeah, my life in my
hands, oh Lord.
Leaving my unborn child—oh Lord, one foot in
the grave.

I am caught on the bridge——in London Town.
Lawd I'd give my life for love—my Andrea.
I got to run—my pressure won't come down.
Hark angel, dark Angel, you will burn in fire.

I hide in the mist and the cold—London Town.

8. WHERE IS MY SUN?
(monologue)
PAPA GILLY

Am I safe from the paw of the law?
Where is my sun, my orb of gold?
Big Ben chimes at the noon of day,
Still, she hides for time untold.
It's a fog over Westminster way.
Damp and chilling, dark and brooding.

Is this summer, or the horrid winter of my
discontent, possibly?
My bed and pillow set low on the floor of the
Seaman's Infirmary.
Yes, I board at the Seaman's syphilis hospital
in Clapham.
They house me like a leftover from the war—a
madman.
Andrea, my love back o'er the Caribbean Sea—
out of sight.
My plight employed to rebuild Britain's great,
great might.

And I like Faust hath sold my soul for a great
cost.
Andrea and my unborn child, all is gone, all
is lost.
Huge chimneys on houses belching smoke like
factories.
To be with my Andrea, I would trade the
queen's riches.
Where is my sun? No sun, no golden sun.
A fog-damp and chilling, dark and brooding.

9. PORTLAND CEMENT

Nig-Nog look.
You're not light like Portland cement.
Not even a legal resident.
You rebuild for the next Jubilee.
London is big, a city for the celebrity.
Building like the Phoenix after the War.
By my knuckle-duster, Sambo, I am a star.

Rebuilding done, go back to your fun.
Oh, island in the sun, your golden sun.
No sun can burn through our London fog.
Someone go on fetch me a proper cup.
Hot tea never last past the first sup.
Britain lasts a thousand years and up.

BECCA

Windham, you are not a politician.
But goodness me, you do sound like the famous
one.

WINDHAM

Britain reigns a thousand years by any shot.
Much longer than the fate of this cursed lot.

10. ISLAND MOVES

London mash up after your big bad war.
England cry out come from near and far.
Goodness Gracious, offer of a lifetime.
Leave the colonies, chance of lifetime.You
need our spirit to get this place lit.
Island move, body groove, get this place lit.

Move over and let us turn London to bright.
Even if you are cement white, get right.
London mash up after your big bad war.
England cry out come from near and far.

You need our spirit to get this place lit.
Island moves, body grooves, get this place
lit.

11. BORN WITH A TAN

Mamma gave me this tan.
Draped in melanin like a sapphire night
without a moon.
It don't mean, I got no feelin', deep in my
soul.
Oh, I can work all night and day without
breaking.
I got this feeling for my wo-man left weeping.
On a sapphire night, without a moon.
Ooh my love, w-a-i-t I'll come soon.

Night and day, I am grieving, in her arms I'd
be rejoicing.
This labor would be light as the island breeze
a-blowing.
And wouldn't I toil as hard as they please? As
hard…
I see my child in my woman's arms.
She is standing where I left her.
On a sapphire night, without a moon.
Ooh my love, w-a-i-t, I'll come soon.

Mamma gave me this tan.
Draped in Melanin like a sapphire night-
without a moon.
Oh, I work all night and day without breaking.
Like the Phoenix I am here for the rebuilding
I got this feelin' for my wo-man left weeping.
Ooh my love, w-a-i-t, I'll come soon.
On a sapphire night, without a moon.

12.RUDE BWOYS NEVER SURRENDER
(Zeke Raps to drumbeat)

Every day we walk in packs to catch the
homebound trains.
Them Teddy Boy gangs will beat you with their
wire chains.
Take this long screwdriver and never
surrender.
I always carry one in my pocket just remember.
Rude bwoys fight for justice and never
surrender

13. COME TO LONDON AND SEE

England welcomes you to her friendly shore.
See a smiling face as you go door to door.
Goodness Gracious, come to London and see
Chance of a lifetime, Goodness Gracious me.
Great Britain is a place I'm longing to see.

I going to Cambridge to be an engineer.
Have no fear, you are welcome over here.
Goin' to Queen's hospital, a nurse I'll be.
Goodness Gracious me, come to London and see.
Chance of a lifetime, Goodness Gracious me.

Have a sip of de Bajan rum,
Dance, but don't tumble down.
Have no fear, you are welcome over here.
Goodness Gracious me, come to London and see.
A chance of a lifetime, Goodness Gracious me.

14. THE VALLEY AT DUSK

You dance like waves rolling to the shore.
I swing with your moves and beg for more.
Light touches your skin, soft as a valley at
dusk
I reach out and touch, soft as a valley at
dusk.

We dance like waves rolling to the shore.
We swing and dance and search for more.
Light touches your skin, soft as a valley at
dusk.
I hold you, soft as the grass in the valley at
dusk.

15. LOVE OF A LIFETIME
(to Latin beat)

How can I, give up on love?
My-a-h love of a lifetime.
And I-ah feel you in my arms.
My l-o-ve of a life-time.

Ti-m-e stops- in your arms.
Nothin' but my beating heart.
Will you ever return-
Nothin' but my beating heart.

My love of a life-time
My love of a life-time
My love of a life-time

How can I, give up on love?
My-a-h love of a lifetime.
And I-ah feel you in my arms.

My l-o-ve of a life-time.
Ti-m-e stops- in your arms.
Nothin' but my beating heart.
My love of a life-time.

16. WORTH IT

If I ever—hold you again—fill my heart with
your love.
The thunder of hammers and the smell of
burning oil
Would cease, and my heart aches no more for
your love.
Brown cocoa skin—twilight on my lonely, lonely
hills.
And this toil in the dungeon of my soul would
be worth it.
Some d-a-y I will see you again and life would
be worth it.

(Tosses his hat and sits on the railroad tie.)
For years, I searched all of England for the
love of my life. As soon as I save up enough
pounds, I will trot off to find my her again,
after all this time. My Edith-Louise…
(sings)

Brown cocoa skin—twilight on my lonely, lonely
hills.
And this toil in the dungeon of my soul would
be worth it.
Some-day I'll see you again and my life would
be worth it.
If I ever—hold you again—I'll fill my heart
with your love
My thunder ceases, and my heart aches no more
for your love.
And my life would be worth it, and life would
be worth it.

17. JERICHO ROAD

Sometimes you take the train down Jericho
Road.
Rebuilding the Great Empire is such a heavy
load.
The lodging they offer is the Seaman's
infirmary.
There is no room in the inn, no room in the
city.
Let not your heart be troubled on this dark
day.
God knows your name and will make a way.

Make your way through the dark and gloom.
My God is bringing light into this very room.
A Phoenix rising, through the fog London—town
Rising through the fire and ash of London
town.

Rebuilding the Great Empire is a heavy load.
There is no room in the inn, no rest in the
city.
Can't lay my head in the sick man's infirmary.
Oh-oh oooh the train down to Jericho Road.

Let not your heart be troubled on this dark
day.
My God knows your name and will make a way.
There is a Phoenix rising up from the ashes.
Up from the dust into the new London Town.

18. LOVE SURPRISE

Aw, Aw love comes as a sur- pr-i-se
Aw, aw fell for those beautiful eyes.
Aw, aw never, never knew you would care.
Aw, aw, love flows here there and everywhere.

Aw, Aw love comes as a sur- pr-i-se
Aw, aw fell for that beautiful smile.
Aw, aw never, never you would care.
Aw, aw love flows here, there, and everywhere.

People dancing in the street.
Everybody rocking to the beat.
                    (rap)
You body, you body movable,
Shake it, make it rumble.
Unzip it, and mek it tumble.

19. MAN'S MUSIC

Reggae's a man's music; Reggae's a man's
music.
A woman's voice don't fit with this acoustic.
Can you leave church, sing with the Rude
Bwoys?
Lost, grumpy men who never had nice, nice
toys.
Can you wear a mini-skirt and swing your hips?
No church music from your sugar, sweet lips.

Reggae's a man's music; Reggae's a man's
music.
You make people dance— your voice of magic.
Can you wear a mini-skirt and swing your hips?
No more church music from your sweet, sweet
lips.

(raps)

Now I can stop my search.
I am taking you out of church.
Found a love that I can feel.
My life here just became real.

20. WOMAN'S MUSIC

Reggae's woman's music; Reggae's woman's
music.
A woman's voice can play with any style
acoustic.
I can sing with better than your rude, Rude
Bwoys.
Lost, grumpy men who never had nice, nice
toys.
I can wear a mini-skirt and swing my saucy
hips.
And sing reggae music from my sugar, sweet
lips.

Reggae's a woman's music; Reggae's woman's
music.
We make people dance— with our voices of
magic.
Can you wear a mini-skirt and swing your hips?
All kinds of music from my sugar-sweet lips.
A woman's voice can play with any style
acoustic.
I can sing with better than your rude, Rude
Bwoys.

(rap)

Now I can stop my search.
We can stay in the church.
Found a love that I can feel.
My life here just became real.

21. LONDON RAIN

Just when I found the looo-ve of my life,
Here comes the rain--London rain,
All over broken, broken heart.
I reach for you babe, and you flit away
Here comes the rain, London rain,
All over my broken, broken heart.

Shadows come like rain London rain,
All over my broken, broken heart.
It rains, like London rain.
Just when I found the love of my life,
Here come the rain, London rain,
London pain, all over by broken heart.

22. A GOLDEN SUN

A golden sun
Yes, finally sun.
It is the light.
Your beautiful eyes

You light my way.
Am I here to stay?
More than today
Our golden sun

I close my eyes.
When I lost my way,
No light of day
But your beautiful smile.

Don't look away,
My brand-new day,
Love shows the way.
Am here to stay.

23. RUDE BWOY WALK

Babe-e-eh
I love your rude bwoy way of walking.
Babe-e-eh
And your Jamaican way of dancing.
But if you are going to be my lover yeah,
You must make me tingle all over babeh
Babe-e-eh
Just give me the finer things of life,
If you want me to be your wife?

Babe-e-eh
I can't be your secret lover,
Y-a-a-y
You can't keep me under cover.
Wo-wow- a-a-a-y
Rude Bwoy, walking.
Rude Bwoy talking.

Babe-e-eh
I am good under the cover.
Yeah
Can y-o-u be my lover?

Babe-e-eh
You must love my rude girl style
Babe-e-eh
You feel my passion all the while?
Yaaay
A girl has a right to claim her love.
Baby I am best anytime you need me.
My Rude Bwoy can you ever love me?

24.FOREIGN LAND

When you return from foreign land,
No one awaits to shake your hand.
Bring a suitcase full of money,
Do, don't mashup, the country.
Yes sah, the pound strong,
Stronger the weak Jamaican dollar.

Deportees get no seven-gun salute.
You mess with the queen, my youth.
Yes sah, the pound strong in the island.
Yes sah, the pound strong in this land.
Rude Bwoy, do, keep your record clean.
My youth don't mess with England Queen.

25. DON'T BE PORTLAND CEMENT

You don't have to be light like Portland
cement.
Rude bwoy, you were al-ways a welcome
resident.
Rebuilding for the great, great Jubilee
London is a big city for the ce-leb-rity.
A Phoenix rising from the great, great War.
Windrush people you are stars, big, big stars.

I don't have to be light like Portland cement.
Rude girl, you were al-ways a welcome
resident.
Rude Bwoys Rebuilding for the great Jubilee,
London is a big, big city for the ce-leb-rity.
Windrush people we are stars, big, big stars.
Windrush people we are stars, big, big stars.